Longman Structural Readers: Plays
Stage 4

Loyalty

Richard Musman

Illustrated by Terence Greer

LONGMAN

LONGMAN GROUP LIMITED
London

*Associated companies, branches and representatives
throughout the world*

First published *1970
New impression *April 1971

ISBN 0 582 53754 1

*Printed in Hong Kong by
Yu Luen Offset Printing Factory*

Longman Structural Readers

It is today widely held that it is the structure of a language, rather than the vocabulary, which causes the greatest difficulty to the foreign learner. The supplementary readers in this series are therefore based on the principles of structure control.

Up-to-date English courses have, at each stage, a certain common content of sentence-patterns. This common content, which will be familiar to the learner at the end of each stage, is represented in the structure tables developed to govern the preparation of the series (see *A Handbook to Longman Structural Readers* for the structure tables and basic vocabulary).

Control of vocabulary is also maintained (as in many existing series of supplementary readers) and one new principle has been introduced. Content words outside the given basic vocabulary but of value in the story are introduced freely within the structural limits by a prescribed process of repetition.

The learner's pleasure in reading is thus increased, and with the strict control of useful structures, the development of a sense of achievement will be aided and the maximum value derived from the practice of supplementary reading.

Titles in this series

P – Recommended for use in the Primary School
S – Recommended for use in the Secondary School
A – Recommended for use with Adult Students

Contents

TO STRIKE—OR NOT TO STRIKE

Note on Trade Unions

A union is a joining together of things or people. A trade is a business which buys, sells or makes things. Workers join together in trade unions in order to get better pay and better working conditions.

The world's first trade unions were started in Britain in the 1830s. Today there are trade unions in most western countries—and in some eastern countries too. Some of these unions are very large and important. Others are quite small. The trade unions have given power to the workers. The greatest of these powers is the power to call a strike—a stopping of work.

Some people in Britain today think that the union leaders have too much power. Some workers think that they are too weak. Often groups of workers in factories start strikes against the advice of the unions. There are a very large number of strikes each year.

What is going to happen to the trade unions? Some people think that the trade union laws ought to change. Many trade unionists are afraid of a change. It is one of today's most important and difficult problems—not only in Britain, but in many other countries too.

Characters

JOCK FRASER
MEG FRASER, his wife
MARY DUNCAN, their daughter
REGGIE DUNCAN, Mary's husband
HAMISH DUNCAN, Reggie's brother
RUTH DUNCAN, Hamish's wife
MRS CHURCH, a schoolteacher

Scene 1

(The sitting-room of the Frasers' house. It is a comfortable room. Jock Fraser is a foreman at a factory which makes motor car parts. It is five o'clock on Monday afternoon. Mrs Fraser is laying the table for supper. Mary is in the passage [the door is on the right]. You cannot see her. But you can hear her voice clearly. She is at the front door.)

MARY *(to her small son)*: Don't be late. Promise! Goodbye!

(You hear the front door shut. Mary comes into the room. She is less than thirty. She married young. But she and her husband still live with the Frasers. Reggie works at the same factory as Jock Fraser. Their one child, Peter, is nine.)

MRS FRASER: Where's he going?

MARY: Peter? He's going to play in the park.

MRS FRASER: Alone?

MARY: He'll meet some of his friends, perhaps.

MRS FRASER: You ought to have another child.

MARY: Reggie says we can't afford it.

MRS FRASER: Of course you could afford it! But Reggie doesn't want another child. He doesn't understand children. He never plays with Peter. He spends all his time at the factory.

MARY: We're trying to save money. We want to buy our own house. You know that, Mum.

MRS FRASER: Is that why Reggie is against the strike—because he wants to save money?

MARY: No, of course not! You know Reggie's ideas about strikes.

MRS FRASER: Reggie has too many ideas! He's as bad as his brother.

MARY: You know that's not true, Mum! Reggie is against strikes. He likes hard work. But Hamish wants to stop all work at the factory. He's against everything. He's against the firm. He's against the Union. If the firm offered Hamish £30 a week, he'd ask for £50. If the Union demanded a thirty-hour week, he'd demand a twenty-hour week. He's only happy when he's causing trouble.

2

Reggie has too many ideas!

MRS FRASER: Your dad thinks that Hamish is right this time. He thinks that the men ought to strike.

MARY: Dad only says that because he's loyal to the Union. He wasn't at all pleased when the Union called the strike.

MRS FRASER: It's good to be loyal. Your dad has belonged to the Union since he was eighteen.

MARY: Reggie is loyal too. He's loyal to the firm. He has worked for the firm since he was sixteen. But Hamish isn't loyal to the firm or the Union. He wants the men to have all the power. And he wants to be their boss. How many strikes did he start last year—against the advice of the Union?

MRS FRASER: Three! And you know what your dad said to him! But this is different. This time the Union called the strike—not Hamish.

MARY: Reggie thinks that the Union's claims aren't fair. He thinks it's a stupid strike. The Union leaders want sixpence an hour more. And they're only asking for it because the bus drivers won their claim last month! That's what Reggie says. And that's what all the newspapers say. The whole country's against the strike. Most of the other unions don't agree with it either.

MRS FRASER: Your dad says that some of the other unions may join the strike.

MARY: But he doesn't want that to happen, does he? If there's a big strike thousands of men in the car factories will have to stop work. The car factories can't continue work without the parts which dad and Reggie make. You saw all those thousands of cars on the telly last night? If there's a strike the factories won't be able to finish them. We won't be able to sell them to foreign countries. We won't be able to get all that foreign money—and we need it badly. Dad and Reggie agree about that. You know they do.

MRS FRASER: Your dad will do what the Union says. He always has done what the Union says.

MARY: The Union leaders can be wrong sometimes, can't they? Reggie wants to leave the Union.

(*The two women have not noticed that the sitting-room door has opened. Mr Fraser and Reggie are standing at the door. They are listening to the conversation. Mr Fraser is a large, quiet man. But today he is unusually excited. His wife notices this as soon as she sees him. She goes to him and takes his coat. But he does not look at her. He is looking at Reggie. Reggie is a small man who moves quickly and talks quickly.*)

MR FRASER: Is this true, Reggie? Are you going to leave the Union?

REGGIE: If there's a strike—yes.

MR FRASER (*angrily*): You'll never understand what the trade unions have done for the working man! You don't know what it was like in the Twenties and Thirties*!

REGGIE: You often tell me, dad! But it's different now. The working man doesn't need help and comfort any more! The unions ought to stop strikes—not start them. They ought to fight trouble-makers like Hamish.

MR FRASER: The workers will always need the help of the unions. Without the trade unions, the bosses could sack workers when they liked.

REGGIE: It would be a good thing if they could! You're a foreman. You ought to be on the side of the bosses. You agree that many men don't work hard enough. The bosses ought to sack men like that—and trouble-makers like Hamish! But they daren't. You remember what that man on the telly said last night? They daren't sack anybody—because they're afraid of strikes.

MRS FRASER: Is there going to be a strike?

MR FRASER: Yes—if the firm and the Union can't agree before Monday.

REGGIE: Well, I'm not going to strike. And I know plenty of other men who won't either.

*Note: In the nineteen-twenties and thirties millions of men were without work. The trade unions called many strikes. Most of the strikes failed. Many families did not have enough to eat. But the unions got more power as a result of the strikes. Older British workers have never forgotten those unhappy days.

MR FRASER: If you go against the Union, there will be trouble at the factory. You know that, don't you? It'll be unpleasant. It may even be dangerous. Hamish and his boys have been waiting for a moment like this.

REGGIE: If we want to go to work next week, nobody can stop us—not even Hamish. We'll call the police, if necessary.

MR FRASER: If you call the police, there really will be trouble.

(*At this moment there is a loud knock on the front door. Mrs Fraser goes to open the door. Hamish Duncan rushes into the room. He is a little older than his brother. And he is larger and has a stronger face. He is the kind of man whom other men like to follow. He is holding a piece of paper. He is very angry. He goes to Reggie. He pushes the piece of paper under his nose.*)

HAMISH: This is your work!

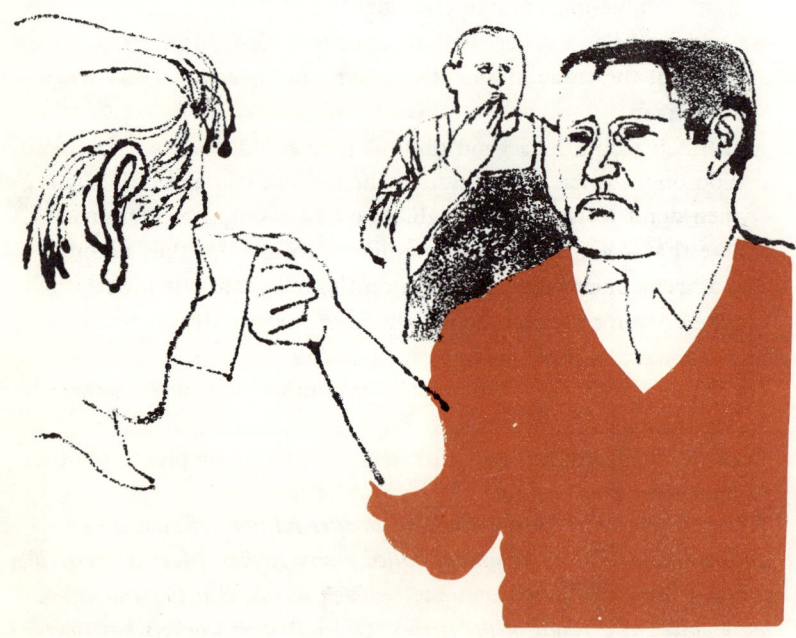

This is your work!

REGGIE (*coldly*): Clearly! It's got my name and address on it!

HAMISH (*very angry*): It's not your business! It's the business of the Union. The Union will decide—

REGGIE: The Union! You don't care what the Union decides. You're always starting strikes against the advice of the Union. I am trying to stop a strike.

HAMISH: You're the bosses' darling, aren't you? You're their favourite. You want a better job. That's why you're doing it. You're doing it for yourself!

REGGIE: Don't say that!

HAMISH: It's a free country, isn't it? I can say what I like.

REGGIE: Yes, it's a free country! So if I want to go to work on Monday, I'll go. And you can't stop me.

HAMISH: I'll stop you, all right! You'll see!

MRS FRASER: Be quiet, both of you! I'm tired of your stupid quarrels. What's that piece of paper?

MR FRASER: It's a voting paper.

MRS FRASER: What for?

MR FRASER: Reggie wants a vote at the factory—to strike or not to strike.

HAMISH: He can have his vote! I'll call all the men together during the dinner hour tomorrow. Then you'll see who wants a strike!

REGGIE: Yes, we'll see! We all know what you'd do. You'd jump on to a table and you'd shout: "Hands up those who are against the strike!" then you'd shout: "Come on! We all want to see you!" And nobody would dare to put his hand up. They'd all be afraid—afraid of you and your friends! They'd remember the boy you pushed into the river last year—because he didn't put up his hand!

MRS FRASER: What kind of vote does Reggie want?

MARY: He wants a secret vote. He's sent one of these papers to every man in the factory. They can write on it "yes" or "no". Then they can post the paper back to Reggie. They won't have to put their names on it. So no one need ever know what they voted.

HAMISH: And no one will ever know if Reggie threw any papers into the fire!

MARY: You think that Reggie wouldn't be honest? He'd never do a thing like that! Reggie paid for those papers. It cost him a lot of money.

MRS FRASER: You're sure that the men want to strike, Hamish. So why are you afraid of a secret vote? I think that a secret vote is a good idea. What do you think, dad?

MR FRASER (*slowly*): Yes, I think it's a good idea. If there was a law, I would agree. But there isn't a law. So Hamish is right. It's not Reggie's business. The Union won't like it

REGGIE: I don't care whether the Union likes it or not!

HAMISH: We'll find out who votes against the strike. We've got names already. (*He turns to Reggie.*) There's yours for a start. You'll pay for this! Oh yes! You'll pay for it!

(*Hamish goes to the door and leaves. He does not even say goodbye.*)

MRS FRASER: What have you started, Reggie? Do you know what you're doing? I hope so. Oh, I hope so!

Scene 2

(*Thursday. The Frasers' sitting-room at nine o'clock in the evening. Mr Fraser is reading the newspaper. Mrs Fraser is sewing.*)

MRS FRASER: Do you think Reggie will win?

MR FRASER: No.

MRS FRASER: But Reggie is right. The whole country is against the strike. Even that paper you're reading says so. And it's usually on the side of the strikers.

(*Mr Fraser does not answer. He continues to read.*)

MRS FRASER: You voted. I saw you put the piece of paper in an envelope. You sent it to Reggie through the post! How did you vote?

MRS FRASER: It's a secret vote, Meg. You mustn't ask me.

MRS FRASER: I know how you voted. You voted for the strike. I don't understand you. You're one of the most important men

at the factory. Everybody listens to your advice. You don't
want the strike. You don't think the Union is right. You
really agree with Reggie. The secret vote gave you your chance.
But you voted on the same side as Hamish. Hamish wants to
destroy the Union. You're always saying so yourself.

MR FRASER: So does Reggie. They both want to destroy the
Union—for completely different reasons. They want a war
inside the Union. And what would happen then? Have you
thought about it, Meg?

MRS FRASER: Reggie wants a secret vote. That's not war. That's
fair.

MR FRASER: Yes. That's fair, Meg. But what will he do if he
loses?

MRS FRASER: We'll know soon. Here they are.

(*You can hear the front door opening. The door shuts loudly. A moment
later the sitting-room door opens and Reggie and Mary come in. Reggie
looks very angry indeed. Mary does not take her eyes off him.*
*Mr Fraser puts down his newspaper. Mrs Fraser puts down her
sewing.*)

MR FRASER: You lost!

REGGIE: By two votes! And one of those votes was yours! You
voted against me, didn't you?

MR FRASER: It was a secret vote—your idea, Reggie. I'm not
telling you.

MARY: You did vote against him! He's your daughter's husband.
So you voted against your daughter!

MR FRASER (*very angry*): Don't you ever say that again! Do I have
to agree with him—just because he has married my daughter?
I don't like that dress you're wearing. We don't quarrel about
that, do we?

REGGIE: That's stupid! Dresses and ideas are completely different.

MR FRASER (*still very angry*): Listen, Reggie! We're living together
in the same house. We have different ideas. We don't have to
quarrel.

MARY: Why are you so angry then, dad?

REGGIE (*to Mr Fraser*): You could stop the strike. You didn't. People like you cause all the trouble in the country. You think that the Unions are more important than the country. You didn't agree with the Union bosses when they called the strike. But you were afraid to quarrel with them.

MR FRASER: I wasn't afraid. I told them what I thought. But sometimes people must accept what they don't like. If the workers aren't loyal to the Unions, they'll destroy the Unions— and themselves. Countries without trade unions can't remain free.

REGGIE: Well, I'm not going to strike!

(*Mr Fraser turns to his wife.*)

MR FRASER: You see, Meg?

MRS FRASER: That's not right, Reggie.

REGGIE: The others can strike if they want to. I won't try and stop them. But I'm going to work on Monday. And they'd better not try and stop me!

MRS FRASER: But you voted, Reggie, and you lost.

(*At that moment there is a loud knock on the door. Nobody moves at first. At last Mary goes towards the sitting-room door.*)

MARY: That's Hamish!

MRS FRASER: Tell him not to start a quarrel, Mary!

(*Mary goes out and opens the front door. There is a sound of voices in the passage. Then Hamish and his wife, Ruth, come into the sitting-room. Ruth is small. She is a little older than Mary. She has a kind, gentle face. Hamish and Ruth have no children. But they have several cats and dogs. Some people say that Hamish is kinder to his animals than to his wife. The Frasers are sorry for Ruth, and Ruth and Mary would like to be friends.*)

HAMISH (*he looks at his brother and laughs*): Well, what are you going to do now? (*Before Reggie can answer he continues.*) Ruth and I were there. We helped to count the papers—didn't we, Ruth?

RUTH (*unhappily*): Yes.

HAMISH: We counted those bits of paper ten times—ten times,

do you hear? We had to! Reggie and Mary can't count! *We* got the right result the first time, didn't we, Mary?

(*Mary looks angrily at him, but she does not answer. Nobody speaks.*)

HAMISH (*to Reggie*): You ought to write a letter to the Union. You ought to say that you're sorry!

REGGIE: I'm going to work on Monday!

HAMISH: What!

REGGIE: Nearly half the votes we counted were against the strike. Nearly half the men didn't send back their papers. Some of those who didn't vote are on my side. So I'm going to play your game, Hamish. I'm going to call a meeting tomorrow. If half the men go to work on Monday, the strike will fail.

(*Hamish is so surprised that he laughs.*)

HAMISH: *You* are going to call a meeting, Reggie? All right! You do that! Call a meeting! I'll be there. We'll all be there. (*He looks at his watch.*) I needn't waste any more time. Come on, Ruth! I'm hungry.

(*He laughs again and moves towards the door.*)

HAMISH: See you tomorrow then—at the meeting!

(*Ruth follows her husband. But at the door she stops.*)

RUTH (*in a quiet little voice*): How's Peter, Mary?

(*Before Mary can answer Hamish laughs loudly.*)

HAMISH: Poor Peter! He's going to be so ashamed! When his friends tell him the news, he'll—

MARY: You leave Peter alone!

HAMISH (*to Mary*): Don't look at me! I haven't got any children. Go and talk to Bill Trevor—and Fred and Tom and Cliff. They've all got children who go to Peter's school. I wouldn't like to be Peter on Monday morning. Oh no! I wouldn't!

REGGIE: I could kill you!

MRS FRASER: The children at school are only babies! Peter will be all right. Mrs Church will look after him.

RUTH: Oh yes! He'll be all right, Mary. Nobody will hurt him.

HAMISH: Don't be too sure, Mary! That young Dickie Trevor is a big boy—

(*Reggie rushes at Hamish. But Mr Fraser jumps up and stands between them.*)

MR FRASER: Get out, both of you! You can fight in the streets, in the factory, if you like. But not in here! Get out, do you hear.

(*The two brothers look at Mr Fraser with surprise. Then Hamish laughs and goes out of the door at once. Reggie does not move.*)

MR FRASER: You too Reggie!

(*Reggie looks at Mary and moves slowly towards the door. Mary starts to follow him.*)

MR FRASER: Come back, Mary!

(*Mary stops and looks at her father with surprise. She sits down unhappily as Reggie shuts the door.*)

RUTH: I'd better go and get Hamish's supper.

(*She goes towards the door. At the door she stops and turns to Mary.*)

RUTH: I'm sorry, Mary. I'm sorry about everything.

Scene 3

(*Friday evening. Mrs Fraser and Mary are in the sitting-room. They are at the table. They are doing nothing and they are not speaking. Sometimes there are footsteps in the street, then their eyes turn towards the door.*)

MRS FRASER: They're late.

MARY: I hope dad will look after Reggie.

MRS FRASER: Look after Reggie? Reggie will have to look after himself. Your dad is still very angry with him. He thinks it's all his fault. Why didn't he accept the result of the vote? A lot of men are saying that Reggie is thinking only of the money. They are saying that he is thinking more of his new house than of his mates.

MARY: That's a lie, Mum!

MRS FRASER: Your dad says it's terrible at the factory now. He says that already two of his mates have quarrelled. And he says that it will be worse—if Reggie calls that meeting.

MARY: Reggie will call the meeting! Why do you always blame

Reggie, Mum? If Hamish wasn't there, there wouldn't be any trouble.

(*The door opens and Mr Fraser and Reggie come in. There is blood on Reggie's coat, and his face is white. Mary gives a cry.*)

REGGIE (*almost angrily*): All right! I'm not going to die!

MRS FRASER: What happened?

MR FRASER: He had a fight with Bill Trevor. Bill knocked him down.

MARY: Did you call the meeting, Reggie?

REGGIE: Yes!

MR FRASER: Reggie called the meeting! But Hamish kept his promise. He and his friends were there. As soon as Reggie opened his mouth, they shouted, they threw things—

MARY (*to her father*): And you just stood there? You allowed it all to happen?

MR FRASER: Yes!

MARY: And when the fight began, you did nothing?

MR FRASER: Nothing!

MARY: But why, dad? You don't like Bill Trevor.

MR FRASER: Reggie said something terrible.

MARY: You didn't stop the fight!

MR FRASER: I'm not the factory policeman!

MRS FRASER: So what's going to happen on Monday?

(*Reggie takes off his coat and gives it to Mary. She is going to take it into the kitchen. But when she reaches the door she stops. She looks at Reggie.*)

REGGIE: I'm going to work on Monday!

MARY: No!

MR FRASER: And how many of your friends are going to the factory with you? Tell them that.

MARY: Yes. How many men will be with you, Reggie?

REGGIE: None of them—the cowards!

MR FRASER: If you go to work on Monday Hamish and his boys will be waiting for you. They could hurt you. You ought to remember your family.

I'm not going to die!

REGGIE: I'm going to the police.

MR FRASER: If you do that, *you* will be the coward. The men are already saying that you're a coward. They are saying that you didn't fight Bill Trevor. You allowed him to hit you. You didn't hit back.

REGGIE: I didn't hit back, because I'm against violence.

MRS FRASER: You say that you're against violence, Reggie. But you often start it—"I could kill you!" Isn't that what you said to Hamish yesterday? What did you say to Bill Trevor today?

MR FRASER: I wouldn't allow him to repeat it—not in front of you. (*He turns to Reggie.*) Mum is right, Reggie. You asked for a fight. I have never seen so many angry men at the factory. If there's trouble, they'll blame you this time—not Hamish.

(*There is a knock at the front door. Mary goes to open it. A moment later Ruth comes in.*)

MRS FRASER (*surprised*): Hullo, Ruth!

RUTH: Hullo, Mrs Fraser! (*She turns to Mary.*) I had to come. Mary, keep Peter at home on Monday.

MARY (*quickly*): Why, Ruth?

RUTH: I was in the park this evening. I heard the children talking. They know that Reggie and Bill Trevor had a fight.

MRS FRASER: They know already?

RUTH: Yes, I'm afraid so. He oughtn't to go to school on Monday.

(*Reggie looks at Ruth angrily.*)

REGGIE: It's not your business, Ruth. Peter will go to school on Monday.

MARY: But why, Reggie? You heard what Ruth said. It's not fair. Children are cruel.

REGGIE: Peter can look after himself.

MRS FRASER: He can't fight the whole school.

REGGIE: Fight? They're only ten year-olds. Mrs Church would soon stop a fight.

MARY: They won't fight, Reggie. They'll laugh at him.

REGGIE: All right! They'll laugh at him. But he can't stay at home for ever, can he?

MARY: You're bringing children into your quarrel, Reggie—our child!

REGGIE: Don't blame me! If there's any trouble at the school, it won't be my fault.

MARY: Yes, it will, Reggie! It *will* be your fault—if Peter goes to school.

(*Reggie turns to Ruth.*)

REGGIE: There wouldn't be any trouble, if Hamish talked to Bill Trevor. Bill Trevor would listen to him. So would the others. But Hamish wants trouble, doesn't he, Ruth? If Peter stays at home, they'll laugh at *me*. They'll say I'm afraid.

(*Mary sits down. She looks unhappily at her mother and father.*)

MARY: Oh, why did you start all this, Reggie?

(*Reggie turns his back and looks out of the window.*)

Scene 4

(*Monday, eleven o'clock in the morning. The Frasers' sitting-room. Mrs Fraser and Mary are at the table. Ruth Duncan is standing at the door. She has her coat on. She has clearly only just arrived.*)

RUTH: Did he go to school then?

MARY: Yes.

RUTH: But why, Mary?

MARY: Reggie took him. He refused to listen to any of us.

MRS FRASER: Before Reggie left the house a message came. It was from Mrs Church. She advised Mary to keep Peter at home. The police had been to see her.

RUTH: So Hamish was right! Reggie did go to the police?

MRS FRASER: Oh yes! He told them everything. Of course the police gave Reggie the same advice as Mrs Church. He refused to take it. So a policeman went to see Bill Trevor and the fathers of other children at Peter's school. The men will never forgive Reggie now.

RUTH: A policeman followed Hamish when he went to the factory this morning. There must be a lot of policemen outside the factory. Where's Mr Fraser?

MRS FRASER: He went early to the factory. But he won't be able to do anything if there's any trouble. Most of the older men have stayed at home.

RUTH: Do you think there will be any violence?

MRS FRASER: Dad doesn't think so.

MARY: Anybody could throw a brick at Reggie.

RUTH: Oh, they wouldn't Mary! They wouldn't!

MARY: Are you sure, Ruth? Hamish once said in this room: "The workers will use violence if they have to!" The police couldn't stop that.

RUTH: But Reggie is his brother!

MARY: Don't be stupid, Ruth! Hamish hates Reggie more than any one in the world. You know that.

(*At that moment Mr Fraser comes in. He takes off his coat and sits down. The women watch him.*)

MRS FRASER: What happened, Jock?

MR FRASER: Nothing—yet. I was right. Hamish and his boys didn't use any violence. They didn't even threaten him. They didn't have to. They formed two long lines on both sides of the gates. And while Reggie walked between them, they laughed at him. "He's a big, strong boy!" they shouted. "He's going to do all the work himself!" They cheered him. "Good old Reggie! Three cheers for Reggie! He's going to save the firm!"

MRS FRASER: So it wasn't as bad as you thought?

MR FRASER: Oh, it was bad—very bad for Reggie! Hamish is clever. He knows that sometimes laughing can hurt more than violence. Reggie will never be able to work in the factory again.

(*Mary gets up and goes towards the door.*)

MARY: I'm going to get Peter.

MR FRASER: No, leave him, Mary. If there's any trouble, Mrs Church will send him home.

(*Mary sits down again. Ruth sits down beside her.*)

MARY (*unhappily*): What are we going to do, if Reggie loses his job? It isn't fair. Reggie was doing well at the factory.

MR FRASER: He'll get another job. He's a good worker. He

They formed two long lines

oughtn't to work in the same factory as Hamish. You oughtn't
to live in the same town

MARY (*angrily*): It's Hamish who ought to leave!

RUTH: Oh, I'm sorry, Mary! I'm so sorry!

(*Suddenly there is a knock at the front door. Mr Fraser gets up and
goes and opens it. Hamish rushes in. He doesn't look at anyone. He
is speaking as he comes through the door.*)

HAMISH: I didn't want this, Mary. How did it happen? Why did
it have to happen? Why? Why?

(*Mary gives a cry.*)

MARY: Reggie! What have you done to him?

(*Hamish looks at Mary. He is so surprised that he can't say anything
at first. He looks at the others. They are all waiting, white-faced.*)

HAMISH (*slowly*): Of course! You don't know! They haven't told
you yet!

MRS FRASER: Told us? Told us what? What's happened, Hamish?

(*Hamish hides his face in his hands. He speaks through his fingers.*)

HAMISH: I can't tell you. The police must tell you. Why aren't
they here?

MR FRASER: You must tell us, Hamish. Look at the women!

(*Hamish looks up. But when he speaks, he isn't looking at anybody.
He stops after each sentence.*)

HAMISH: It's Peter. He was running across the road. A bus hit
him.

MARY (*cries*): Where is he?

(*She rushes towards the door, but Hamish pulls her back.*)

HAMISH: No. You mustn't go! I've seen him. He's dead!

(*Nobody speaks. Everybody is looking at Hamish. They do not seem
to understand. Suddenly Mary runs out of the room. You can hear
her climbing the stairs. There is the sound of an upstairs door
shutting. Still nobody speaks.*)

HAMISH: Don't look at me like that! It wasn't my fault, I tell you!

MRS FRASER (*in a very quiet voice*): We're not thinking of you,
Hamish! Where did it happen?

HAMISH: In front of the school. I didn't see the accident. I was outside the factory. I heard the noise. I heard people shouting. I went to see.

MR FRASER: How do you know he's dead, Hamish?

HAMISH (*cries*): How do I know? Don't ask me! I saw him lying in the street.

MRS FRASER: I'll go to Mary.

(*She is leaving the room when there is a knock on the front door.*)

HAMISH: That'll be the police.

RUTH: I'll open the door, Mrs Fraser.

(*Mrs Fraser sits down. Her husband goes to her and puts his arm round her. Hamish does not move. A moment later Ruth appears at the sitting-room door.*)

RUTH: It's Mrs Church. Can she come in?

MR FRASER: Of course.

(*Mrs Church is a small woman. She is not young. She has a soft voice. She stands at the door and looks around her. Clearly she is looking for Mary.*)

MR FRASER: My daughter has gone to her room. You can understand, after the terrible news—

MRS CHURCH: Yes, indeed.

MR FRASER: Sit down, Mrs Church. It would be better if Mary didn't hear yet. But please tell us. We'd like to know.

(*As Mrs Church sits down she sees Hamish.*)

MRS CHURCH: You're Hamish Duncan, aren't you, Peter's uncle?

HAMISH: Yes.

MRS CHURCH: You haven't any children, have you?

HAMISH (*almost angry*): No. Why do you ask?

MRS CHURCH: The children were shouting your name this morning. (*She turns to the others.*) Peter arrived at school. Two or three of the older boys began to laugh at him. I saw his father in the street. I ran after him. I told him that Peter ought to go home. But Mr Duncan was rather rude to me. He said he was in a hurry. He had to get to work.—Did Mrs Duncan get my message?

MR FRASER: Yes. My daughter tried to keep Peter at home.

HAMISH (*to Mrs Church*): You said that the children shouted my name. What did they say?

(*Mrs Church does not seem to notice Hamish. She continues.*)

MRS CHURCH: Little Dickie Trevor started it. He said to Peter: "My dad knocked your dad down at the factory yesterday! Your dad's a coward!"

(*Now Mrs Church turns towards Hamish.*)

MRS CHURCH: Were you at the Trevors' house yesterday evening, Mr Duncan?

HAMISH: Yes, I was. Bill Trevor is a friend of mine.

MRS CHURCH: And did you say—in front of Mr. Trevor's children—"My brother has always been a coward?" (*Hamish is going to say something, but Mrs Church continues quickly.*) You did say it, didn't you, Mr Duncan?

I'll kill you

HAMISH (*in a very quiet voice*): Yes, I said it. (*Then suddenly he is very angry.*) But why did you allow the boy to run across the road? Why didn't you look after him properly? I hope they sack you!

RUTH: No, Hamish! No!

HAMISH: Be quiet, you!

(*Mrs Church turns to Mr and Mrs Fraser.*)

MRS CHURCH: I stopped them at once. We began the lesson. The children forgot Peter. They worked well. Then the telephone rang. I had to leave the class. It was Peter's father. He was phoning from the factory. He wanted to know if Peter was all right. (*She pauses.*) I got back to the classroom. All the children were standing on their desks—except Peter. He was standing alone near the door. They were pointing at him and shouting: "Coward! Coward!" They stopped as soon as they saw me. But it was too late. Peter ran out of the door, across the playground and into the street. There was nothing that I could do.

(*Suddenly the door opens and Reggie rushes in. He sees Hamish. He raises his arm and takes a step towards him.*)

REGGIE: The police told me what happened. I'll kill you—

(*Then he sees Mrs Church. Mrs Church is looking at him. Their eyes meet. Reggie lowers his arm, stops and falls into a chair. He covers his face with his hands.*)

THE PLAN

Characters

WAR MINISTER
HIS WIFE
BELLA, their daughter
TINA, secretary to the War Minister
STILO
PILTIN

Scene 1

(*The sitting-room of a large house. The house is just outside the capital city of a small country. It belongs to the War Minister. The War Minister, his wife and daughter are fixing black curtains across the tall windows* [*centre*] *which lead into the park. The door is on the left. There is a clock on the wall beside the windows. The hands of the clock are pointing to six o'clock. It is getting dark. The War Minister is a small man of fifty-five or sixty. He has not much hair and he is rather fat. His round face is kind, but not especially clever. He is a family man who enjoys his comforts and loves his family. The War Minister's wife is fifty, more or less. Her grey hair is untidy. She is wearing a black dress which fits her badly. Clearly her duties as mother and wife are very important to her. You would be surprised if she read books, or even newspapers. You would be even more surprised if she understood her husband's work. She has the look of a friendly but not very brave bird. Their daughter, Bella, is eighteen or nineteen. She is gay and well dressed. She is fond of her mother and father. But quite clearly she knows that she is cleverer than either of them.*)

BELLA (*jumps to the floor from a tall pair of steps*): There! That's finished. They're not very pretty, are they?

WIFE (*to her husband*): Do you think they're really necessary, dear?

23

Do you think we'll win this war?

WAR MINISTER: I'm afraid so. (*He looks at the clock.*) In two hours the war will begin.

BELLA: Because they threw bad eggs at our ambassador? Is that why we're going to fight?

WIFE: They've thrown eggs at him nine times during the last week!

BELLA: But is that why we're going to war, father?

MINISTER: There are other reasons, of course!

BELLA (*laughs*): I'd like to throw eggs at the ambassador myself. He's an ugly little man. And he thinks he's so important!

MINISTER: You mustn't talk like that, Bella darling. He's—well, he's like our flag.

BELLA (*laughs again*): Our flag is the ugliest flag in the world! Do you think we'll win this war, father?

MINISTER: Of course!

BELLA: We've never won a war before.

MINISTER: No. (*He looks around him and lowers his voice.*) But this time we've got a plan. It's very secret. When the enemy attack, they will get a surprise—a terrible surprise. Our army won't even have to fight. The plan will save the lives of hundreds of our soldiers. (*He looks at the clock again.*) In five hours, perhaps four hours, the war will be over.

BELLA: What is the plan, father? Tell us!

MINISTER: I can't tell you, my darling. It's secret.

BELLA: How many people know this secret plan?

MINISTER: Only myself, the First Minister, the generals—and Tina, of course.

BELLA: Tina knows it? Why Tina?

MINISTER: Because she's my secretary. She doesn't know what's in the plan, of course. She just knows there is one.

WIFE: If we're going to win this war so easily, why are you sending us both into the country? I don't understand, dear. We'd much rather stay with you.

MINISTER (*he puts his arms round his wife and daughter*): My darlings, I wouldn't be happy if you stayed here. You know that. The enemy have a few aeroplanes. They may attack the city as soon as the war starts. I want to know that you are safe. You will be quite safe in the country.

WIFE: But you've sent the servants into the country too. There will be no one to look after you, to cook your meals.

MINISTER: We must all serve our country!

BELLA (*she kisses her father*): Father, you're sweet! I hope the plan is a good one!

MINISTER (*very seriously*): Oh yes! It's good!

(*At this moment there is a knock at one of the windows. They look at the window with surprise.*)

BELLA: What was that?

WIFE: A knock at the window!

MINISTER: My gun is in my bedroom.

(*He is going to run out of the room. But his wife stops him.*)

WIFE: Don't leave us alone! Oh! Why aren't the servants here!

BELLA: I'm sure it was the wind. I'll go and see.

MINISTER: No! No! There isn't any wind. I'll go myself.

Scene 2

(*He pulls back the black curtains and opens one of the windows. A girl comes in. She is wearing a heavy leather coat. She has one hand in her pocket. She looks round the room quickly.*)

MINISTER: Tina! What are you doing here? And why didn't you ring at the front door?

TINA: I'm in trouble, Minister. I need your help. Are you alone?

MINISTER: You can see. There's only my family.

TINA: There is nobody in the house? You're quite sure? No one must see me. No one must know that I'm here.

MINISTER: The servants have all gone.

TINA: There are no soldiers in the park?

MINISTER: No, just two at the street gate, and another two at the country gate. (*When he says "country gate" Tina smiles suddenly.*) But why all these questions, Tina? What's the matter? Of course we'll help you, if you're in trouble. You can go with my wife and daughter into the country. They're leaving soon.

TINA(*suddenly*): No, Minister, they can't leave! None of you can leave.

MINISTER: But why, Tina? What's happened? Why are you looking at me like that?

(*Tina does not answer. She goes to the window, opens it and calls.*)

TINA: Stilo! Piltin! You can come in now.

(*Two men come in. They are dressed in black. They are both carrying guns. The older man* [Stilo] *is small and thin. He has a thin nervous face. When he moves, he moves nervously. When he talks, he talks nervously. His eyes move around the room all the time. The younger man* [Piltin] *is tall and large. He has a pleasant face. He holds his gun like a man who understands guns. But he does not look dangerous. When Bella and her mother see the guns they give a cry. The Minister's face is white, but he stands bravely in front of his wife and daughter.*)

MINISTER: What do you want? Explain, Tina!

(*Tina does not answer. She looks at Stilo.*)

STILO (*to Tina*): Get three chairs. Put them by the wall over there.

(*Tina places the three chairs by the wall. Stilo turns to the Minister and his family.*)

STILO: Sit down on the chairs. That's right! In a straight line, like at school! Now Minister, we'll tell you why we're here. We want the plan!

MINISTER (*turns to Tina*): Did they threaten you, Tina? (*Tina does not answer.*) They're not your friends! You're not—

STILO: Yes, Minister. Didn't you know? She's working for us!

WIFE: (*to Tina*): He was like a father to you!

(*Stilo puts the gun against the Minister's head.*)

STILO: We're in a hurry. Tell us the plan!

MINISTER: No!

STILO: We'll kill you, if you don't—slowly in front of your family. No one will hear the shots. (*He points at his gun.*) Our guns have silencers.

WIFE: Tell them!

MINISTER: No!

WIFE: You must! You must!

MINISTER: No! If I tell them, hundreds, perhaps thousands of our soldiers will die. It's my life or the life of all those men. I can't do it. You mustn't ask me to. My life isn't important.

WIFE: It's important to us. You belong to us. You belong to your family.

STILO: You're wasting our time. Are you, or are you not going to tell us the plan? Your family will watch you die slowly. It will not be pleasant for them.

MINISTER: They will have to be brave.

BELLA (*suddenly*): You won't kill my father—not yet! If you kill him now, you won't get the plan. You're just threatening him.

(*Stilo takes the gun from the Minister's head. He laughs unpleasantly.*)

STILO: You've got a clever daughter, Minister! She's quite right. If we killed *you*, we'd never get the plan. Tina told us you were a brave man—not very clever, she said, but brave! "He won't talk if you threaten *him*," she said. "But try his family!"

(*Stilo goes quickly to Bella and puts the gun against her head. Bella gives a cry and puts her hands in front of her face. The Minister tries to jump up. But Piltin pushes him back into his chair.*)

MINISTER (*to Stilo*): You wouldn't!

STILO: Wouldn't I? Have you forgotten what we did to the ten hostages last December, Minister?

TINA: I read the report to you! Don't you remember, Minister? They were all shot, and two of them were women.

STILO: Now your wife and daughter are hostages!

MINISTER: You're barbarians!

STILO: *We* have soldiers, too, Minister. Their lives are worth more to us than the lives of your wife and daughter. I'll kill your daughter—slowly, if necessary—in order to save the lives of our soldiers.

MINISTER (*very quickly*): All right, I'll tell you!

WIFE: Oh yes! Tell them. You must tell them. Look at his eyes! He's cruel. He'll kill her if you don't tell them.

BELLA: Oh no! Oh no! You can't, father!

MINISTER: I'll tell you! You won't hurt her, if I tell you? You promise?

Your wife and daughter are hostages

STILO: Yes! Yes! Hurry!

(*The Minister speaks with a great effort. He stops after each sentence.*)

MINISTER: We will allow your army to take the first village. The village will be empty. The people have already left. As soon as your army appears, our army will leave too. They will run. They will not fight. You understand?

STILO: Yes! Yes! They never fight! They always run!

(*The Minister agrees sadly.*)

MINISTER: So when our soldiers run, you will not be surprised. But you will stop in the village, because our army will leave behind all its stores and all its guns—

STILO: And then?

MINISTER (*very slowly*): We have bought from a foreign power a new and very powerful explosive. It is hidden in the middle of the village. There is an electric wire which leads to a hill outside the village—on our side of the village, you understand?

PILTIN: Yes, we understand very well!

(*It is the first time that Piltin has spoken. The Minister and his family look at him with surprise.*)

MINISTER: At the right moment we will press a button. (*His voice is so quiet that it is difficult to hear him.*) The explosive will destroy everything in the village. Your army will be completely destroyed.

PILTIN: You called us barbarians!

MINISTER: It's war!

(*Stilo pushes Bella's head back with his gun. She gives a cry.*)

STILO: And shooting hostages is also war!

MINISTER: You can make peace. There needn't be a war. We have several of these explosives. They are in different parts of the country—along the roads which lead to the capital. You cannot win the war. You—

STILO: The different places where these explosives are hidden! They're all on the plan! Isn't that right?

MINISTER: Yes.

STILO: Where is the plan?

MINISTER: There is a copy in my office at the Ministry.

STILO: You haven't got a copy here? (*He presses the gun against Bella's head again.*)

MINISTER: No! No! It's true. I—

STILO: Then you will go and get the plan. Your family will stay here. (*He looks at the clock on the wall.*) If you don't bring us the plan before seven o'clock, we will shoot your wife and daughter. Listen carefully. Your car is at the door. You can reach the Ministry in ten minutes. Tina will go with you. (*He stops and takes out of his pocket two very small boxes. He shows them to the Minister.*) They're radios, very special radios. Tina will take one of them. (*He gives one to Tina.*) The other one will stay with me—here, in this room. (*He places the second radio on the table which stands on the right of the room.*) If you betray us, Tina will send a signal with her radio. We will then kill your wife and daughter at once.

MINISTER: But there are soldiers at the Ministry. The rooms are full of people. There is a soldier in my office all the time. If Tina talks into her radio, someone will see, someone will hear—

TINA: Explain to them, Stilo!

(*Stilo turns to the radio on the table. He presses a button. Immediately there is a "pip, pip" noise. It is not loud. But you can hear it quite clearly. Then Stilo turns to Tina.*)

STILO: Now give the signal, Tina.

(*Tina presses a button on her radio. Suddenly the "pip, pip" noise of Stilo's radio changes to a loud, unbroken buzz. Almost a quarter of a minute passes before anybody speaks. They are all looking at the radio on the table.*)

STILO (*at last*): You see, Tina won't have to talk.

(*He presses the button on his radio. At once the loud buzz changes back to the quiet "pip, pip" noise. This noise continues while they talk. You can hear it each time there is a pause*)

STILO (*to the Minister*): That was the signal!

(*He points his gun first at Bella, then at her mother.*)

STILO: We won't wait. We will kill them at once—at once, do you hear?

WIFE: No! No! (*To her husband.*) You must bring back the plan. We can win the war without the plan. You must save us!

STILO: She's right! You must bring back the plan!

MINISTER: Will you promise not to hurt my wife and daughter?

PILTIN (*quickly*): Yes. We promise.

(*Stilo looks at the clock.*)

STILO (*to Minister*): It's getting late. Get up and walk in front of Tina to your car. If you betray us, you will die too. Tina has a gun.

WIFE: Oh no!

(*Tina takes a small gun out of her pocket.*)

TINA: Come on, Minister, walk! Stay in front of me all the time. Don't turn round. Don't look at me. Just walk to your car and drive me straight to your office.

MINISTER: You, Tina! I don't understand!

BELLA (*suddenly*): How much are they paying you, Tina?

TINA (*turns angrily to Bella*): That's none of your business!

(*Stilo pulls Tina by the arm.*)

STILO: You're wasting time. Leave now!

(*The Minister takes one step, then he stops.*)

MINISTER: But what will I say if someone stops me? My voice, my face will tell them that something is wrong. You know me, Tina—

TINA: Yes, I know you, Minister! You must say: "I can't wait. I'm in a hurry." You say that every evening when you're returning to your family! We'll practise in the car! Hurry!

(*Stilo pushes the Minister out of the room. Tina follows him. As Tina reaches the door, Piltin suddenly calls.*)

PILTIN: Be careful, Tina!

(*Tina turns and looks at him.*)

TINA: I'll come back!

WIFE (*as the door closes*): Come back quickly!

Hurry!

Scene 3

(*As soon as they have gone, Stilo sits on the table beside the radio. Piltin stands in front of the two women. But he does not look at them.*)

WIFE: He was like a father to her! She was very sick last year. One night I sat beside her bed. I was there all night. We gave her presents—

PILTIN: Be quiet!

BELLA: Is she your girlfriend?

PILTIN: That's not your business!

(*Stilo does not move from the table. His eyes are on the radio. There is a pause. The "pip, pip" noise seems very loud.*)

BELLA: She is your girlfriend, isn't she? I saw your face when she left. I saw her face too. Are you going to marry her—if ever you get back to your country alive?

PILTIN: I've told you! That's none of your business!

BELLA: Must we sit here on these hard chairs? My mother's not very well—Didn't Tina tell you?

WIFE: Yes. I'm not very well.

(*Piltin looks round at Stilo.*)

BELLA: Won't you allow her to sit on a more comfortable chair?

(*Piltin does not speak.*)

STILO (*looks up*): No!

BELLA (*to Piltin*): Is he your captain? Do you always do everything that he says?

(*Piltin does not answer.*)

BELLA: Will he really kill us if my father does not bring the plan?

PILTIN (*quickly*): The plan! Are you proud of the plan? Are you proud of your father?

(*Bella looks at her mother, then at Piltin, then at the radio. The "pip, pip" sound seems louder than before.*)

BELLA (*slowly*): No, I'm not proud of the plan. I think it's terrible. But my father's War Minister. He had to do his duty. He had to try to win the war, didn't he? He's not a cruel man—

PILTIN: I know that kind of man! He could press the button which will kill ten thousand men. But he couldn't stick a knife into a woman—not even into Tina!

WIFE: Oh no! He couldn't! He couldn't!

BELLA (*to Piltin*): You couldn't either! Your friend could, but you couldn't. If Tina presses the button on her radio—(*She pauses. They all look at the radio on the table.*) if Tina gives the signal, your friend will try and kill us. But you won't help him. You'll just stand there. No! You won't even do that. You won't want to see. You'll turn your head—

PILTIN: Be quiet!

BELLA: Yes, you'll turn your head. But you'll have to watch. You'll have to listen. What will happen—when the signal goes? My mother and I are not brave. We'll jump up. We'll run all over the room. Your friend will have to shoot many times before he kills us both.

WIFE: Don't talk like that, Bella!

34

BELLA (*continues*): We'll scream. There'll be blood all over the place. You won't like to see a woman's blood, will you? Have you ever heard a woman scream with fear and pain? Have you ever seen blood before? No. You're too young. You weren't in the last war!

PILTIN (*shouts*): Be quiet!

(*Stilo gets up from the table and comes to Bella. He presses the gun against her head.*)

STILO: Yes. Be quiet! Or I'll shoot you!—*now*!

WIFE: Don't! Don't!

PILTIN (*to Stilo*): No!

(*Piltin does not touch Stilo. But Stilo lowers his gun. Nobody talks. The only sound in the room is the "pip, pip" of the radio.*)

BELLA (*to Piltin at last*): You see, you're not any better than my father. You promised my father that you would not kill us. (*She points at Stilo.*) He almost killed me. I was so afraid that I couldn't even scream. But you did nothing—nothing at all!

(*Stilo does not threaten Bella this time. He turns to Piltin.*)

STILO: Tie her to the chair! Put a cloth in her mouth!

(*Piltin takes a step towards Bella. She pushes her chair right back against the wall.*)

BELLA: No! No! If you touch me, I'll scream. There may be soldiers in the park. Yes! The soldiers sometimes come into the park.

(*Stilo goes to her. He raises the gun above her head. Bella puts her arm in front of her face and gives a cry of fear. At the same time Piltin pushes Stilo back.*)

WIFE: Don't hurt her! Don't hurt her! She doesn't understand. She's only a child.

PILTIN (*to Stilo*): If you hurt her, the Minister may cause trouble. He may destroy the plan in front of our eyes.

STILO: All right! I won't hurt her—yet! (*To Bella.*) You said that soldiers sometimes come into the park. How often?

BELLA: I don't know. A soldier from one of the gates sometimes comes. He walks round the house.

(*Nobody talks while Stilo goes to the window. The "pip, pip" sound of the radio fills the room. Stilo pulls back the black curtain very carefully and looks through a small hole.*)

STILO (*at last*): I can't see anything. I can't hear anything. I think you're lying. I don't believe—

(*He is just walking back to the table when suddenly the "pip, pip" sound stops. As all eyes turn towards the radio, the signal comes— the long unbroken buzz. At first nobody moves. Nobody speaks. Then Stilo looks at the clock.*)

STILO: They left less than four minutes ago! (*He turns to Bella.*) How far is it to the street gate?

BELLA (*she speaks so softly that you can only just hear her*): Half a mile.

STILO: Then he has betrayed us to the soldiers at the gate!

WIFE: It must be a mistake. (*She screams and points at the radio on the table.*) That terrible noise! Stop that terrible noise!

(*Stilo picks up the radio and throws it on the floor. The noise stops at once.*)

PILTIN: They must have caught Tina. I'm going to find out.

STILO: Come back!

(*Piltin moves towards the door. But Stilo holds his coat and pulls him back. Piltin suddenly sits down on a chair. Stilo pushes him.*)

STILO: Get up!

(*But Piltin does not move.*)

STILO: Tina was wrong! (*He shouts.*) Your girlfriend was wrong, do you hear? That fool of a War Minister has betrayed us. The plan is more important to him than his family. Tina made a mistake. So she must pay for it. (*He turns towards Bella and her mother.*) And so must they!

WIFE: It's not possible! It's not possible!

STILO (*to Piltin*): Get up! Show the girl she was wrong. Kill her! Tina would want it.

PILTIN (*gets up slowly*): No. We won't get the plan now. So it's not necessary to kill them.

STILO: You fool! They'll kill Tina. Perhaps she's dead already. (*He points to the two women.*) So we'll kill them. They're our hostages. We're at war. If we don't kill them, we'll never be able to take hostages again.

PILTIN (*he speaks slowly*): I don't care. I'm not going to kill the girl. And I won't allow you to kill her either—or the mother.

(*Pilton and Stilo are now face to face in the middle of the room. Their guns are in their hands, but at their sides. The two women watch.*)

STILO (*at last*): You soft fool! (*He raises his gun.*)

PILTIN: Be careful! I can shoot quicker than you.

STILO: You'd kill me? You're on their side?

PILTIN: I'm not on their side. But I won't allow you to kill them.

STILO: Why? Why?

PILTIN (*he points at Bella*): Because she was wrong. I have seen people die. The other hostages were shot. I was there. I saw them die—one after the other. The women were shot last. I watched their faces while their husbands died. I watched their faces, do you hear? They screamed when their turn came.

WIFE: Oh!

STILO (*shouts*): Then why are you here? You only came to look after Tina, didn't you? But Tina doesn't need your help. She's not soft like you. *She'd* shoot them.

PILTIN: Perhaps. But I can't.

STILO: And you'd shoot me?

PILTIN: If you try and shoot them, yes!

STILO: You'd shoot me in the back? Oh no, you wouldn't! You're soft. You couldn't kill a fly.

(*He turns quickly and faces the women. As he raises his gun the wife screams and Bella throws herself on the floor. Suddenly Stilo drops his gun. His hand goes to his back. He takes a step forward. You then notice Piltin's gun. Smoke is coming from it. As Stilo falls to the ground, he gives a cry.*)

STILO: You've done it! Traitor!

Scene 4

(*The Minister's wife hides her face in her hands. Bella jumps up. She goes down on her knees beside Stilo. Piltin does not move. He is still*)

He's dead!

holding his gun. But it is hanging at his side.)

BELLA (*looks up at Piltin*): He's dead!

PILTIN: I'm not a traitor. I had to do it.

(*At this moment the door opens. Piltin does not move. He does not even look round. The Minister comes in. He is breathing heavily. He is holding a gun. As soon as Bella sees her father, she goes to him.*)

BELLA: Father!

(*The Minister points his gun at Piltin.*)

MINISTER: Drop your gun and put your hands up.

(*Piltin drops his gun. But he does not put his hands up. He just stands where he is. The Minister puts his arm round Bella. But his eyes are still on Piltin.*)

MINISTER: Put your hands up. Go and stand over there—against the wall.

(*Piltin puts his hands up, but he does not go over to the wall.*)

PILTIN: What happened to Tina?

MINISTER: She's dead. Go over to the wall.

(*Piltin drops his arms. He hides his face in his hands. The Minister is going to move towards him. But Bella stops him.*)

BELLA: She was his girl, father.

MINISTER (*sadly*): I didn't want to kill her.

(*He suddenly notices Stilo's body.*)

BELLA: He's dead, father.

(*During all this time the wife has been sitting on the chair. She has not really understood what has been happening. Now words begin to flow from her like a river.*)

WIFE: He was going to kill us. He was going to kill us. He pointed his gun at us. What happened? What happened? I don't understand. But he was going to kill us. I saw his eyes. They were cruel, cruel!

(*The Minister forgets about Piltin. He goes and sits beside his wife. He puts his arm round her.*)

MINISTER: It's all right, dear. Everything is all right.

PILTIN (*to Minister*): Why did you kill her? I didn't kill your daughter.

(*Bella picks up Piltin's gun. But she does not point it at him. She puts it on the table.*)

BELLA: That's right, father. He saved our lives. (*She points at Stilo's body.*) He shot him. What happened, father? Why did Tina send the signal?

(*The Minister puts down his gun, and passes his hand across his eyes. He looks very tired.*)

MINISTER: We were driving towards the street gate. I wasn't driving fast. But I was nervous. You can understand that, can't you? I hit a tree. It wasn't serious. We weren't hurt. But Tina fell forward. The radio in her pocket hit the side of the car. The button was pressed. The signal was given. I didn't know it because no sound came from the radio. Even Tina didn't know it at first. But then suddenly she found out. She told me! I was sure that they would kill you. I forgot everything. I tried to get out of the car. I wanted to run back to the house at once. But Tina took out her gun. She shouted at me: 'Drive on! You must get the plan. If you don't drive on, I'll kill you!' (*He looks at Piltin.*) She wanted to kill me. You know that, don't you? But I didn't care any more. I thought my family was dead. I took her arm before she could shoot. We fought in the car. She's a strong girl. She hit me. She bit me. And all the time she held the gun. Then suddenly she was quiet. I saw that there was a hole in her leather coat above her heart. I could see blood. I called her name. She didn't answer. I didn't wait. I took her gun and drove straight back here.

(*Piltin runs to the door. But the Minister jumps up. He picks up the gun and shoots above Piltin's head. Piltin stops and turns towards the Minister.*)

PILTIN: Perhaps she's still alive!

MINISTER: No. She's dead.

PILTIN: I want to see her.

MINISTER: No. Sit down (*Piltin sits down on a chair on the other side of the room.*) You ought to be glad that she died like that. You know what we would have done to her!

40

(*Nobody speaks. At last Bella points at Piltin.*)

BELLA: What are you going to do to him, father?

MINISTER (*surprised*): Do to him? Call the police. (*He gets up and walks to the telephone.*) I'd better do it at once.

BELLA: No, father! Don't phone. Does anybody know what happened—except us? Did the soldiers at the gate see?

MINISTER (*he has his hand on the receiver*): No, nobody. Why?

BELLA: Father I think the plan is terrible. It's wicked!

MINISTER: War is wicked. We all know that.

BELLA: This is different, father. I would never forgive you, if you pressed that button. I would never forgive you if you destroyed all those men.

MINISTER: It's too late, Bella. I can't stop it now.

WIFE: You don't understand these things, Bella. You're only a child.

BELLA: You can stop it, father. If this young man goes back to his country, he can tell them about the plan. They won't know where the explosives are. But they'll know the danger. They won't dare to make war. You can stop the war, father. (*She looks at the clock.*) We have more than an hour. (*She turns to Piltin.*) I don't know how you came into our country. But how long did it take you?

PILTIN: Less than an hour.

MINISTER: But the soldiers at the gate won't allow him to pass, Bella. He was only able to get in because Tina was driving.

BELLA: *We* will take him out, father—you and I. And we'll take Tina, too. She can go home with him.

WIFE   No, Bella!
                (*together*):
MINISTER   But, Bella—

BELLA: I will drive, father. (*She points to Piltin.*) We'll take his car. He can lie on the floor in the back. You can sit on the back seat with the gun. (*She lowers her voice.*) Tina will sit beside you in the back. It's dark. The soldiers at the gate won't notice anything. (*She suddenly notices Stilo's body.*) We can't leave him here. And Mother can't stay alone. We'll put him in the boot of the car—Mother, do you feel strong enough to drive *our* car?

WIFE: No! No! You mustn't go in the car with that man. I won't allow it. It's too dangerous. No! I won't drive our car.

BELLA: Then you'll have to stay here alone, mother. I'm sorry, but—

WIFE: How can you talk like that, Bella! You're only a child (*She looks at her husband, but he turns his head.*) Very well, I'll drive the car.

BELLA: There's a large wood a mile from the country gate. We'll change cars in the wood. (*She points to Piltin.*) He'll drive on to his country in his car. We'll drive home in our car. We can stay at home with father now, mother. There won't be a war.

MINISTER: I can't do it, Bella. I can't betray my country.

BELLA: You're not betraying your country, father. You're stopping a war.

MINISTER: Your mother is right, Bella. You're only a child. You don't understand these things. Everyone will say that I betrayed my country.

BELLA: No one will ever know, father. (*She points to Piltin.*) He won't say where he got the news.

(*Piltin has his head in his hands. He says nothing. He does not even look up.*)

MINISTER: Of course he will! He's our enemy. He'll say what he likes.

BELLA: No, he won't. If he does, we'll tell everything. We'll say that he killed his friend. (*She goes to Piltin.*) You want to save your soldiers, don't you? You'll try to get home? You want to take Tina home, don't you?

(*Piltin looks up.*)

PILTIN: Yes.

MINISTER: No, Bella. I can't do it. If I betray my country, I shall remember it for the rest of my life.

(*Bella suddenly picks up the gun from the table. She points it at her head.*)

| WIFE | (*together*): | No, Bella! |
| MINISTER | | Give me that gun, Bella! |

Decide, Father

BELLA: You say that I'm only a child, father. But if you
don't agree, I shall kill myself. I shall! You haven't really
thought, father. The plan is wicked. If you press that button
I won't want to live any more.

(*The Minister does not say anything. Bella looks at the clock.*)

BELLA: Decide, father. We haven't got much time.

(*The Minister takes his hand off the receiver. Then he takes his wife's
arm, and they walk out of the room together. Bella puts the gun down
on the table and looks at Piltin. Piltin gets up slowly. The Minister
returns and stands in the door. He is holding his gun again.*)

BELLA (*to Piltin—she points at Stilo's body*): Is there room for him
in the boot of your car?

PILTIN: Yes.

(*Piltin begins to lift Stilo as the curtain falls.*)

HE'S NOT A FRIEND OF MINE

Characters

MR FELLOWS

MRS FELLOWS

BEN FELLOWS

JUNE FELLOWS

MIKE STANDING

POLICE INSPECTOR

POLICEWOMAN

MACGREGOR, a policeman

Scene 1

(*A back sitting-room in the East End of London. The door which leads into the passage is in the centre* [*right*]. *The door which leads to the kitchen is in the centre* [*left*]. *Where the passage door opens, you can see the bottom of the stairs. You turn right in the passage to the front door. It is a poor man's house. Through the window* [*left*] *you can see a small garden, and a high black wall beyond it. There is no view of the sky. There is a sound of ships in the distance. It is six-thirty, and it is almost dark. Mr and Mrs Fellows are sitting at the table in the centre. They have almost finished their supper. There are two empty places.*)

MR FELLOWS: Where's that boy?

MRS FELLOWS: He's in his room. He says he doesn't want any supper.

(*Mr Fellows gets up. He is a big, ugly man. He is not wearing a coat and his white shirt is dirty. He has a loud voice and eyes which never smile. He goes to the door which leads to the passage. He opens the door.*)

MR FELLOWS (*shouts*): Ben! Come down here!

(*A few moments later Ben appears. He is nineteen. He is well dressed. He is wearing narrow trousers and a blue shirt without a tie. His hair is long, but not too long. He is small, but good-looking. His face is*

44

What's the matter, Ben?

unhappy. If you looked at him closely, you would say that he was always unhappy. He sits down at the table, but he does not touch the food.)

MRS FELLOWS: What's the matter, Ben? Why don't you want your supper?

(*Mrs Fellows' hair is grey. Her clothes are grey. Her face is grey. She looks very tired: she is the kind of person you would not notice in a crowd.*)

BEN: I'm not hungry, Mum.

MRS FELLOWS: Aren't you feeling well? You're white.

BEN: I'm all right. Leave me alone, Mum.

MR FELLOWS: Don't talk to your mother like that! Did you see Mr Wills this afternoon? Did he offer you the job?

BEN: No.

MR FELLOWS: Did you see him?

BEN: No.

MR FELLOWS: What! He promised you a good job—£15 a week. We need the money.

BEN: I'll go tomorrow.

MR FELLOWS: Tomorrow'll be too late. I told you. A lot of boys want that job.

MRS FELLOWS: Why didn't you go, Ben?

BEN: I didn't have enough money for the bus. I forgot to ask you this morning.

MR FELLOWS: You're lying! You didn't want the job. You'd rather play records all day in your room.

MRS FELLOWS: I think he's not well, Jack. Look at his face.

(*At this moment June comes in. She looks eighteen or nineteen. She has fair hair. She is wearing a raincoat and a very short skirt. She has a soft, pretty face.*)

MRS FELLOWS: You're very late!

JUNE: I'm sorry, Mum. There has been a robbery in Stanley Street. I stopped and talked to people.

MRS FELLOWS: A robbery! What happened?

JUNE: A man climbed through the back window of an old man's

46

house. He stole some money. The old man found him there.
So he hit the old man on the head.

MR FELLOWS: Have the coppers caught him?

JUNE: Not yet. But a woman saw him leave the house. The police have taken her to the station. She says she has seen him before.

MR FELLOWS: Women! They always help the coppers!

MRS FELLOWS: She was right! Hitting an old man! There would be fewer crimes if more people helped the police.

MR FELLOWS (*shouts*): You're wrong, woman! There'd be more crimes! *I*'d kill anybody who helped a copper! Nobody ought to help a copper!

BEN: Is—is the old man very ill?

JUNE: I don't know. The doctor is still with him.

MRS FELLOWS: Why don't you take off your coat and sit down. I'll get your supper.

JUNE: I haven't got time, Mum. I'm going out with Mike.

(*When he hears Mike's name, Ben looks up quickly.*)

MRS FELLOWS: You're always going out with that boy!

MR FELLOWS (*turns angrily to his wife*): Why not? Mike's her boy-friend, isn't he?

MRS FELLOWS: I'm afraid so, yes.

MR FELLOWS (*very angry*): Afraid so! He's Bert Standing's son, isn't he? The Standings are our best friends.

MRS FELLOWS: Perhaps. But I don't like Mike.

MR FELLOWS: You don't like him because he spent a month in prison.

MRS FELLOWS: He went to prison because he stole a car.

MR FELLOWS: He didn't steal it. He went for a ride in it. That's not a serious crime.

BEN: Where are you meeting Mike, June?

JUNE: That's my business.

MR FELLOWS: When's Mike going to marry you, girl?

JUNE: I don't know. I've told you a hundred times.

MR FELLOWS: I'm seeing his dad tonight in the pub. I'll ask him.

JUNE: Why can't you leave us alone?

MR FELLOWS: We had the idea before you were born, Bert and I!

JUNE (*angry*): Oh, I know! You married us twenty, twenty-five years ago! In the desert during the war! While you were fighting! You're always telling us. We're both tired of it.

BEN: Tell me where you're meeting Mike.

JUNE: Why? What's the matter?

BEN: I just want to know.

JUNE: Mike won't like it if I tell you. You know that, Ben.

MR FELLOWS: Mike has got a good job. I was at Pratt's garage the other day. Mike knows more than Mr Pratt. Mr Pratt said so himself.

MRS FELLOWS: Mike may have a good job, but he loses all his money at the races.

MR FELLOWS: That's his business. Losing money at the races isn't a crime! His dad goes to the races. I go to the races. It's our money. (*He looks at Ben.*) We *work* for it!

MRS FELLOWS: Ben will get a job soon.

MR FELLOWS: Well, why didn't he go and see Mr Wills today?

MRS FELLOWS: He's not well, Jack. Look at him! Can't you see? He's as white as chalk.

MR FELLOWS: If he's ill, why doesn't he say so? Are you ill, or are you just ashamed?

(*Ben does not answer. June smiles at her brother. But he does not look at her.*)

JUNE: Well, I must go. Leave some supper for me, Mum.

(*She goes into the passage. The front door shuts. Mr Fellows gets up and puts on his coat and his cap.*)

MR FELLOWS: Come on, Mary! You'd better come to the pub with me tonight. (*Mrs Fellows begins to pick up the dishes.*) No! Leave them. Ben can wash up. If he stays at home, he can work for his food.

MRS FELLOWS: He hasn't eaten any food! You go to the pub alone, I'm going to look after Ben. He ought to go to bed. (*She puts her arm round Ben.*) Go upstairs, Ben. I'll bring you a hot drink when you're in bed.

BEN (*quickly*): No, Mum. I'm all right. I'd like to wash the dishes.
   Go with dad to the pub. I'll eat something later. I promise you.
(*He gets up and begins to carry the dishes into the kitchen.*)
MR FELLOWS: Hurry up, Mary! Leave him.
(*Mrs Fellows puts on her coat slowly. She does not want to leave.
She watches Ben as he carries a pile of plates through the kitchen
door. Her husband takes her arm and pulls her towards the front door.*)
MR FELLOWS: Come on, Mary! Bert's waiting.
MRS FELLOWS: Take your hands off me!

Scene 2

(*Mrs Fellows goes out of the room in front of her husband. The front
door shuts. Ben comes into the sitting-room. He waits a few moments.
Then he goes to the front door and opens it. He looks up and
down the street. He shuts the door again and goes and stands at the
foot of the stairs. He does not move. His eyes are on the stairs. The
only noise is the sound of the clock above the fireplace. Suddenly he
shouts up the stairs.*)
BEN: You can come down now, Mike. They've all gone.
(*A few moments later Mike Standing comes into the sitting-room. He
is tall and you notice at once his large, strong hands. He is very
good-looking, but his face is unpleasant. He is wearing narrow trousers
and a grey shirt. The shirt is torn and dirty and there is blood on it.*)
MIKE: What did you tell them?
BEN: Nothing. Where were you going to meet June?
MIKE: Outside the cinema—the Rialto.
BEN: And only June knows?
MIKE: Yes.
BEN: You lied to me. That blood on your shirt isn't yours. Why did
   you hit the old man?
MIKE: He began to shout. I was afraid.
BEN: Did the old man see your face?
MIKE: No. I had tied a handkerchief round it.
BEN: But you weren't wearing the handkerchief when you left.
   A woman saw you. The police are questioning her at this

49

Why did you hit the old man?

moment. They'll find out quickly who you are. They'll go to your house. After that they'll come here. They know you're June's boyfriend.

MIKE: They know *you*'re my friend too!

BEN: You're not my friend. I've never liked you.

MIKE: Do you think the police will believe that? We went to school together. I often come to the house.

BEN: Are you threatening me?

MIKE: No. I've told you. I'll give you half the money if you help me.

BEN: And I've told *you*. I don't want your money.

MIKE: You've already got it! I've hidden it in your room. (*Ben moves towards the stairs.*) Don't waste your time. You'll never find it. If the coppers catch me, I'll tell them where it is. I'll tell them that you hid it.

BEN: So you *are* threatening me!

MIKE: Listen, Ben! If I go to prison, you'll go too. We'll go to the same prison—you and me together. You'd like that, wouldn't you?

BEN: The police know you. They wouldn't believe your story.

MIKE: The coppers don't like you much either, Ben. You remember that party we had at the Rialto the other night? You were taken to the station—with the rest of us. And they'll talk to people. Everybody knows what your dad thinks of you. They'll find out you've got no work—or money.

BEN: What do you want?

MIKE: Hide me in your room!

BEN: The police will come straight here. They'll search the house.

MIKE: They'll have to get a warrant first.

BEN: That won't be difficult. They'll get a warrant at once— because you're June's boyfriend.

MIKE: When the police come, I'll climb out of your window on to the roof. When they've gone, I'll climb back again. The coppers won't look far. They know I'm not a fool. Only a fool hides in his girl-friend's house.

BEN: Mum and Dad would find out, and June too.

MIKE: You can tell your dad, if you like. He'd help me. He hates coppers.

BEN: Mum wouldn't help you! She'd like to see you back in prison.

MIKE: You keep her out of your room for two days. I only need two days. I've got a friend on a ship which sails on Wednesday. I'll escape over the roofs at night.

BEN: Do you want to see June before you go?

MIKE: Of course not, you fool! She couldn't keep a secret.

BEN: You don't love her!

MIKE: Love her? Of course I don't!

BEN: She loves you.

MIKE: That's her fault!

BEN: You're a——! (*There is a knock at the front door.*) That's the police!

MIKE (*he runs to the door which leads to the passage*): Remember what I said. I'm going up on the roof.

Scene 3

(*Ben waits while Mike runs upstairs. Then he goes slowly into the passage. You can hear him opening the front door.*)

MAN'S VOICE: Are you Ben Fellows? May we come in? We're police officers.

(*A moment later two police officers come into the sitting-room, a man and a woman. Ben follows them. He keeps his eyes on the ground. The policewoman is in uniform. She is neither young nor old. She has a kind face. But you would try not to disagree with her. The policeman is not in uniform. He is an inspector. He is wearing an old raincoat and an even older hat. He is a small man. He has a soft, almost gentle voice. But when he talks to you, he never takes his eyes from your face.*)

INSPECTOR: Are you alone? Are your mother and father out?

BEN: Yes. They're at the pub.

POLICEWOMAN: Is your sister in?

BEN: No.

INSPECTOR: Where is she?

BEN: I don't know. She never tells me.

(*The inspector walks round the room. He opens the kitchen door and looks in.*)

BEN: Don't you need a search warrant to do that?

INSPECTOR (*stops and looks at Ben quickly*): Where did you learn that word, son? Do you know why we're here?

BEN: No.

INSPECTOR: I think you do! You're a friend of Mike Standing, aren't you?

BEN: No!

INSPECTOR: But you know him!

BEN: Yes.

INSPECTOR: Because he's your sister's boyfriend?

BEN: If you know the answers, why do you ask the questions?

INSPECTOR (*takes Ben's arm and looks straight into his eyes. His voice is less soft than usual*): Think carefully! When did you last see Mike Standing?

BEN (*turns his head*): I can't remember. I never see him unless I have to.

INSPECTOR (*he drops Ben's arm. He smiles. He clearly knows that Ben is lying*): You don't like Mike Standing?

BEN: No. I've already told you. He's not a friend of mine.

INSPECTOR: Then why are you together so often?

BEN: We go to the same parties.

INSPECTOR: Like that party in the Rialto cinema the other evening?

BEN: I only made a noise. I didn't break anything.

INSPECTOR (*softly—after a moment*): All right, son. We'll forget that. May we sit down.

BEN: If you have to.

(*The Inspector sits down in an armchair in front of the fireplace. He lights his pipe. The policewoman sits down at the table. She takes a pencil and a notebook out of her pocket. Ben stands by the door.*)

INSPECTOR: Don't try to leave us. There are policemen outside! Sit down. I want to talk to you.

(*Ben sits down slowly on a chair in front of the Inspector.*)

INSPECTOR: You're not working, are you?

BEN: No.

INSPECTOR: Are you looking for work?

BEN: Yes.

INSPECTOR: What kind of work?

BEN: I'd like to work in a garage.

INSPECTOR: You like cars?

BEN: I like motor-bikes better.

INSPECTOR: Mike Standing works in a garage, doesn't he?

BEN: Yes.

(*The Inspector makes clouds of smoke with his pipe. He does not say anything, but he watches Ben through the smoke. Ben moves uncomfortably on his chair.*)

INSPECTOR (*at last*): How long has your sister known Mike?

BEN: Since she was born.

INSPECTOR: Your father and Mike's father are friends?

BEN: You know they are! Everybody knows that dad and Bert Standing won the war together in Africa.

INSPECTOR (*again he waits a moment before he speaks*): Why don't you like Mike Standing, Ben? What kind of boy is he? You must know him well. You see him a lot.

(*Ben is now very nervous. He opens and closes his hands and moves his feet. He looks at the policewoman. She does not raise her eyes. He looks at the door. He does not speak.*)

INSPECTOR: Have you lost your tongue, boy? You seem very nervous. What's the matter?

BEN (*angrily*): Why are you asking me all these questions? Do I have to answer?

INSPECTOR (*suddenly, and his voice is almost threatening*): Where were you at four o'clock this afternoon?

BEN (*so quickly that the Inspector looks at him with surprise*): Here— in this room.

INSPECTOR: And you didn't leave the room during the afternoon?

BEN: Only to get some cigarettes. You can ask at the shop on the corner. That was at ten to four. I came straight home. Mrs Simons next door saw me come in. You can ask her. She came back from the corner with me.

INSPECTOR: Was it necessary to tell me all that? Why did you tell me?

BEN: I know coppers. They try to trick you. I've seen it on the telly.

INSPECTOR (*sits forward*): Listen, son. This isn't the telly. This is real—very real. At four o'clock this afternoon someone hit an old man in Stanley Street on the head, and took £20 from his house. You knew that, didn't you?

BEN (*after a pause*): Yes.

INSPECTOR (*quickly*): How did you find out?

BEN (*after another pause*): My sister told us.

Why are you asking me all these questions?

INSPECTOR (*quickly*): Your sister! How did she know?

BEN: Her bus-stop is at the end of Stanley Street. The police were there when she came home this evening. She stopped and talked to people. She was late for supper.

INSPECTOR: When did she leave to meet Mike?

BEN (*he doesn't see that the Inspector is trying to trick him*): She left at once. She didn't even take her coat off.

INSPECTOR (*quickly*): So she did go to meet Mike? You lied to us. Why? You knew where your sister was going.

(*Ben does not answer.*)

POLICEWOMAN: Where was she going to meet him?

BEN: At the Rialto cinema.

POLICEWOMAN: At what time?

BEN: At seven o'clock, I think.

INSPECTOR: Did your sister tell you where she was going to meet him? Or did Mike?

BEN: My—sister told me.

(*The Inspector notices the look of fear in Ben's eyes.*)

POLICEWOMAN: Shall I send a car to the Rialto?

INSPECTOR: Yes. Then come back.

(*The policewoman leaves the house.*)

INSPECTOR: You understand now why we're here? When did you last see Mike Standing?

BEN: You won't trick me this time! I've already told you. I can't remember.

INSPECTOR (*very quickly*): Trick you? You don't lie very well, Ben! I repeat: when did you last see Mike Standing? Helping a criminal is a serious crime. You could go to prison.

BEN: I'm not a criminal. You won't frighten me.

INSPECTOR: I'm not trying to frighten you. I'm trying to help you. You're not a criminal—yet. But Mike Standing is a criminal, and a dangerous one too.

(*The policewoman returns.*)

POLICEWOMAN: A girl is coming down the road. I think it's the sister.

INSPECTOR: Good!

POLICEWOMAN: What shall we do?

INSPECTOR: Nothing. Just wait.

Scene 4

(*Nobody speaks. There is the sound of an outside door opening. A moment later June comes in. She has clearly been crying. She looks at the Inspector and the policewoman, then at her brother.*)

JUNE: Why are they here? (*Ben looks at the Inspector.*)

INSPECTOR (*to Ben*): Tell her!

BEN: They think that Mike did the job in Stanley Street.

JUNE (*at once*): He didn't! Of course he didn't.

INSPECTOR: How do you know, Miss Fellows? Did he tell you— at the Rialto, for example?

JUNE (*looks with angry surprise at Ben*): What did you tell them?

BEN: Nothing. I don't know anything. Do you?

JUNE: Yes. I know he didn't do it.

INSPECTOR (*to policewoman*): Talk to her. We'll go into the kitchen.

BEN: You haven't got a warrant.

INSPECTOR (*looks at Ben with surprise*): A warrant? You've used that word before. I'm not going to search the house—or ought I to?

(*Ben does not answer.*)

INSPECTOR (*smiles*): I don't need a warrant to talk to you in the kitchen. You can make me a cup of tea. I'm thirsty.

(*The Inspector and Ben go into the kitchen.*)

POLICEWOMAN (*to June*): Sit down. Take your coat off. Don't be frightened. I only want to ask you a few questions.

(*June sits down, but she does not take off her coat.*)

POLICEWOMAN: Are you in love with Mike Standing?

JUNE: Yes.

POLICEWOMAN: How old are you?

JUNE: Eighteen.

POLICEWOMAN: And how old is he?

JUNE: Twenty.

POLICEWOMAN: And you meet a lot?

JUNE: Yes.

POLICEWOMAN: Has he offered to marry you?

JUNE: No, not yet. But he will.

POLICEWOMAN: How do you know?

JUNE: Because he's in love with me.

POLICEWOMAN (*after a pause*): Your brother doesn't like him.

JUNE (*surprised*): Did he say so? No. He doesn't like him. He doesn't understand him.

POLICEWOMAN: Are you fond of your brother?

JUNE: Yes.

POLICEWOMAN: Is he fond of you?

JUNE: Yes. I think so.

POLICEWOMAN: You're good friends? You tell him your problems?

JUNE: Sometimes.

POLICEWOMAN: When Mike stole that car, did you talk together then?

JUNE: That wasn't a serious crime! The man had three cars! He was very rich.

POLICEWOMAN: Did you make that excuse to Ben? Did he agree with you?

JUNE: No. We quarrelled about it.

POLICEWOMAN: You don't think your brother ought to help the police? If he knew where Mike was, oughtn't he——?

JUNE: Ben would never betray Mike!

POLICEWOMAN: June, Mike hit an old man on the head and stole his money.

JUNE: Mike didn't——

POLICEWOMAN: We know it was Mike. A woman saw him. He also dropped this in the house. (*She takes a brightly coloured handkerchief out of her pocket. June gives a cry. The policewoman puts the handkerchief back in her pocket.*) Helping the police to find a dangerous criminal isn't——wrong.

JUNE: Ben would never betray Mike! Never! I know he wouldn't! Mike's father is dad's best friend.

He dropped this

POLICEWOMAN: We'll find him, you know.

JUNE: He didn't do it! I'm going. You can't stop me!

POLICEWOMAN (*coldly*): You can go, June. We won't stop you.

(*June gets up and runs out of the room. A moment later the front door shuts loudly. The policewoman goes to the kitchen door and knocks. The Inspector comes out and shuts the door behind him.*)

POLICEWOMAN (*surprised*): Can you leave him in there alone? The garden—

INSPECTOR: He won't leave. If he does, he won't get far. (*He points out of the window.*) That wall's twenty feet high. Where's the girl?

POLICEWOMAN: She's gone. Wilson will follow her. I think she's going to Standing's house. You saw her face when she heard the news? It was a terrible shock. She doesn't know where he is, I'm sure of it.

INSPECTOR: Did you find out anything?

POLICEWOMAN: Yes. I think so. She's quite sure that her brother would never betray her boyfriend. She and her brother are good friends. I think Ben Fellows does know something.

INSPECTOR: I'm sure he does. The boy isn't very clever, but he's honest. He didn't help Standing to steal the money. He didn't even know that he was going to do it. But he has seen Standing since the crime. And he is certainly helping him now. Where? How? Why?

POLICEWOMAN: Why? Because Mike Standing is his sister's boyfriend and the son of his father's best friend. He thinks it's his duty. I don't expect he likes coppers, either. Do you think he's hiding Standing here?

INSPECTOR: It's possible. Mike Standing may think that we wouldn't search this house. Phone the station. Ask for more men. I've got an idea.

(*The policewoman leaves. The Inspector goes to the kitchen door and opens it.*)

INSPECTOR: Come in here, Ben.

(*Ben comes in and sits down on the same chair. The Inspector doesn't say anything. He is waiting for the return of the policewoman. At last she comes in. She gives the message to the Inspector with her eyes. Then she sits down again at the table.*)

INSPECTOR (*very suddenly*): We know that you're hiding Mike Standing here, Ben!

BEN (*too quickly*): How do you know?

INSPECTOR (*looks at policewoman and smiles. The trick has worked!*): That's our business! Now tell us where he is. (*Ben does not answer.*)

INSPECTOR: If you're hiding him here, he won't be able to escape. (*He points at the policewoman.*) This officer has just phoned the station. There will soon be policemen all round the house. (*Ben still says nothing.*)

INSPECTOR: You don't like Mike Standing. Why are you trying to save him? Do you want to go to prison yourself?

BEN (*suddenly angry*): Are *you* threatening me too?

INSPECTOR (*quickly*): Did *Mike* threaten you? So you're helping him because you're afraid of him! You're more afraid of him than of the police!

BEN: I'm not afraid of him! But I'd rather go to prison than betray a mate.

INSPECTOR: He's not your mate.

BEN: He's my sister's boyfriend!

INSPECTOR: And if he married her, would you be pleased?

BEN: He'll never marry her! He said so.

POLICEWOMAN: I don't understand, Ben. You'd be very unhappy if he married your sister. He's not your mate. Then why are you helping him?

(*Ben does not answer.*)

POLICEWOMAN: Your sister and your dad would say that you had betrayed him! You're afraid of that, aren't you? But how will you feel if Mike Standing escapes? He may hit another old man on the head.

(*Ben still does not answer.*)

INSPECTOR: Or is it the money? Has he given you some of the money?

BEN: No! (*suddenly stands up.*)

INSPECTOR: Yes! I think you have got the money. (*He takes a £5 note from his pocket.*) You need money, don't you? You're out of work, boy! But the police pay informers. And police money is safe money!

(*The policewoman looks at the Inspector with surprise. She is going to say something. But the Inspector holds up his hand. At the same time Ben jumps up.*)

BEN (*shouts*): You're right! He did offer me money. But I wouldn't take it. He has hidden it in my room.

INSPECTOR: Go and get it.

BEN: I don't know where it is. (*The Inspector holds up the £5 note again.*) I tell you! I don't know! I don't want his money. And I don't want your money either. I'm not an informer. You can keep your dirty money, both of you!

INSPECTOR (*quietly*): Where is he, Ben?

BEN (*sits down again and hides his face in his hands*): On the roof.

INSPECTOR: How did he get there?

BEN: He climbed through the window of my room.

INSPECTOR (*to policewoman*): There are only five houses on this side. I want four men on the roof tops—two at each end of the street.

POLICEWOMAN: Yes, sir.

Scene 5

(*As the policewoman leaves, there are shouts at the front door. Then Mr and Mrs Fellows come in.*)

MR FELLOWS (*looks at Ben in the chair, then at the Inspector*): What has he done?

INSPECTOR: He has helped us, Mr Fellows.

MR FELLOWS: That's no answer. Why are you in my house? Have you got a warrant?

MRS FELLOWS (*runs to Ben and puts her arm around him*): What's the matter, Ben?

BEN (*angrily*): Leave me alone, Mum.

(*At this moment there is a noise on the stairs. Ben jumps up. The Inspector runs to the door. He opens it quickly. Mike Standing is at the bottom of the stairs. The Inspector takes Mike by the arm and pulls him into the sitting-room.*)

INSPECTOR: You'd better come quietly.

(*Mike sees Ben. He looks at him with hatred and points at him.*)

MIKE: *He* helped me. The money's in his room. I'll show you.

INSPECTOR (*turns to Ben*): Where's the money, Ben?

BEN: I've told you. I don't know.

MIKE (*very quickly*): He's lying. It's under the floorboards at the foot of his bed. *He* put it there!

INSPECTOR (*pulls Mike with him into the passage. You can hear him opening the front door. He calls*): MacGregor! (*A policeman arrives.*)

MACGREGOR: Sir?

INSPECTOR (*to Ben*): Which is your room, son?

BEN: The one on the right at the top of the stairs.

INSPECTOR (*to MacGregor*): Look under the floorboards at the foot of the bed. Bring down what you find.

(*MacGregor goes upstairs*)

MR FELLOWS (*to the Inspector*): Show me your search warrant!

INSPECTOR: Take care, Mr Fellows! (*He points to Mike.*) This man has been hiding in your house—with stolen money. Did you know he was here? Did you know that he stole the money from the old man in Stanley Street?

MR FELLOWS (*frightened*): Of course I didn't!

MIKE (*points to Ben*): He told me the money was there. He even told me how much.

MR FELLOWS (*moves angrily towards Ben. But the Inspector stops him*): Now I know why you lied at supper! Now I know why you didn't see Mr Wills!

INSPECTOR (*suddenly turns to Mrs Fellows*): Mrs Fellows, if you learned that your son was a thief, would it surprise you?

MRS FELLOWS: Ben a thief? He'd never steal anything. I've left money in the kitchen, on the table in the bedroom. He's never taken a penny. (*She suddenly points at Mike.*) But that boy's a thief. He steals money from his mother. He'd steal it from his father if he dared. He steals things from shops. I know, because his mother tells me. He once hit his mother—

MR FELLOWS (*shouts*): Be quiet, Mary!

MRS FELLOWS: It's true.

(*MacGregor comes into the sitting-room. He is holding some bank-notes.*)

MACGREGOR: £20, sir. I've counted them.

INSPECTOR (*to Mike*): Come on, you! We're going to the station.

BEN (*to the Inspector—with hope*): Aren't you going to take me to the station?

(*The Inspector does not answer at once. He looks at the Fellows family—one after the other.*)

INSPECTOR (*to Ben at last*): I don't know yet, son. I'll have to think. But don't leave the house. Nobody must leave the house.

There'll be a policeman outside. (*He looks at Mr Fellows.*) Your son did the right thing. (*He takes two more steps. Then he stops and turns to Ben.*) You'll have to give evidence in court. You know that, don't you?

(*The Inspector and Mike leave. As soon as they have gone Mr Fellows rushes towards Ben. But Mrs Fellows stands between them.*)

MR FELLOWS (*to Ben*): You helped the coppers! You'll give evidence in court against Bert's son. You'll send him to prison. You betrayed him!

MRS FELLOWS: Ben did the right thing. The Inspector said so.

MR FELLOWS: He's a copper! Why did you tell him all those stories? They're family secrets.

MRS FELLOWS: They're true. I wanted to help Ben.

MR FELLOWS: You helped the coppers. Nobody ought to help the coppers.

BEN (*suddenly*): The coppers caught *you* once, didn't they, dad? That's why we moved to London. What did you do, dad? Why don't you like the coppers? Did *you* hit an old man on the head?

MR FELLOWS (*in a threatening voice*): Be quiet or I'll give you a beating!

BEN: You won't give me a beating. You wouldn't dare. There's a copper outside! I'll tell you why I helped the police. Mike is dangerous. That policewoman said so. If he had escaped, one day he would have hit another old man on the head. But he's Bert Standing's son! So you make excuses for him. You never make excuses for me! You know Mike's bad. But you want June to marry him. I don't want June to marry him!

MR FELLOWS: You went to the police. Nobody in my family ever went to the police.

BEN (*to his mother*): What did dad do, Mum? Why did we move to London?

MR FELLOWS: Don't tell him, Mary. It's not his business.

MRS FELLOWS: It *is* his business. I will tell him, Jack. (*To Ben.*) Your father hit a policeman in a pub. He hurt the policeman badly. He was sent to prison.

64

MR FELLOWS: Nine months in prison for hitting a copper! Coppers oughtn't to come into pubs.

MRS FELLOWS: You hit another man first, you remember? There was a fight and you began it. They had to call the police.

MR FELLOWS: Why did they have to call the police? It was a fight among friends. We didn't need coppers.

MRS FELLOWS: You were breaking glasses and chairs. I was there!

MR FELLOWS: I was breaking glasses. I wasn't breaking the law. You can pay for glasses.

MRS FELLOWS: But someone who steals other people's money is breaking the law! Someone who hits old men on the head is breaking the law!

MR FELLOWS (*shouts*): Would *you* go to the coppers if *I* hit an old man on the head? Would you betray your husband? Answer me!

(*He takes a step towards his wife. Ben rushes between them.*)

BEN: Get back! Listen, dad! Mike wasn't my *husband*!

MR FELLOWS: He was your mate!

BEN: He wasn't my mate. He was the son of *your* mate. That's different.

MRS FELLOWS (*to her husband*): You'd call for a copper if somebody attacked you!

(*Mr Fellows is suddenly quiet. He sits down on a chair.*)

MR FELLOWS: What am I going to say to Bert? What'll he think? He'll never want to see us again.

MRS FELLOWS: What's the old man thinking—the one that Mike hit on the head? I'd like to know that.

(*There is a sound at the front door. They are all quiet. They wait while the door opens. June comes in. The policewoman follows her.*)

MR FELLOWS: What has she done? Is she in trouble too?

POLICEWOMAN: She has some bad news. Be kind to her.

(*The policewoman leaves.*)

MR FELLOWS (*before June can speak*): Your brother betrayed your boyfriend to the coppers!

(*June sits down on a chair. She is very white.*)

BEN: I'm sorry, June. I had to do it.

I'll never marry him now

JUNE: Yes!

MR FELLOWS (*angrily*): Mike is your boyfriend. You're going to marry him.

JUNE: I'll never marry him now.

MR FELLOWS: Of course you will! He'll be out of prison in a year. Well, perhaps, two years. You can wait for him. You're both young. It's the first time he's been in court—well, the second time. He took a car the first time. But that wasn't serious. He wanted a ride. The court won't be too hard on him—

JUNE (*shouts*): Be quiet, dad! The old man is dead. Mike killed him. Mike is a murderer!

STRESS AND INTONATION EXERCISES

X = stressed syllable
x = lightly stressed syllable
' = a syllable with level stress follows
` = falling tone
´ = rising tone

To the pupil: Your teacher will say each sentence first. Listen to
your teacher. Then say the sentence three times.
Example:

    TEACHER It's 'good to be `loyal.
    PUPILS   It's 'good to be `loyal.
                 It's 'good to be `loyal.
                 It's 'good to be `loyal.

(a) *6 syllables*
Stress Pattern: x X x x X x

It's 'good to be `loyal.
He 'looked at his `brother.
She 'follows her `husband.
My 'daughter has `heard it.
I 'saw them and `heard them.

You'd 'jump on a `table.
We 'helped you to `count them.
He 'oughtn't to `say it.
The 'children for`got it.
They 'started to `hurry.

Stress Pattern: x X x x x X

He's 'loyal to the `firm.
The 'Union will de`cide.
You 'voted for the `strike.
He's 'asking for a `fight.
But 'Reggie is his `friend.

He 'wants to be their `boss.
You 'did it for your`self.
And 'one of them was `yours.
There 'mustn't be a `fight.
The 'men were at the `gate.

Stress Pattern: x x X x X x

She is 'less than `thirty.
He's a'gainst the `Union.
A po'liceman `heard them.

He's as 'bad as `Hamish.
But you 'often `start it.
He's your 'daughter's `husband.

68

They des'troy the `Union.
You can 'hear her `climbing.

Mrs 'Church will `stop them.
We be'gan the `lesson.

Mixed Patterns

A: 'Why did they `laugh at him?

B: Be'cause he was `crying.

A: 'Which of them `started it?

B: 'Little Dickie `Trevor.

C: 'Who are they `voting for?

D: For 'Reggie or `Hamish.

C: 'How are they `doing it?

D: On 'pieces of `paper.

(b) *7 syllables*

Stress Pattern: x X x x x X x

My 'gun is in my `bedroom.
The 'village will be `empty.
He 'thinks that he can `do it.
She 'promised to be `quiet.
I 'hope that it's a `good one.

Your 'family will `watch you.
He 'had to do his `duty.
They 'left it in the `office.
I 'wanted her to `know it.
He'd 'rather be a `soldier.

Stress Pattern: x x X x x X x

There's a 'plan in my `office.
We can 'do it with`out you.
They must 'give us their
    `promise.
He al'lowed us to `help him.
I would 'never for`give you.

You can 'hear it on `Sunday.
You must 'promise to `listen.
He was 'going to `kill us.

We were 'driving to `London.
It's a 'list of the `soldiers.

Mixed Patterns

A: 'Why are they at`tacking us?

B: Be'cause we are `enemies.

A: 'Why are we a`fraid of them?

B: I'd 'rather not `answer you.

C: We've de'cided to `kill you.

D: But 'why are you `telling us?

C: Be'cause we are `gentlemen.
D: Then 'do it im`mediately.

(c) *8 syllables*
Stress Pattern: x X x X x x X x

I'd 'like to 'work in a `garage.

He's 'never 'taken a `penny.

His 'face is 'very un`happy.

You'd 'better 'go to your
`bedroom.

She'd 'like to 'see you in `prison.

I 'think she's 'going to `tell him.

Your 'father 'hit a po`liceman.

I'll 'go and 'see him to`morrow.

He 'came and 'sat in the
`kitchen.

He 'learnt the 'questions and
`answers.

Stress Pattern: x X x X x X x x

He 'says he 'doesn't `want any.

I'll 'tell them 'where the `money
is.

You 'wanted 'June to `marry
him.

You 'didn't 'look at `anyone.

My 'father 'chose the 'best of
them.

I 'only 'want to `look at it.

Your 'brother 'doesn't `answer us.

She 'knows that 'Mike's a
`murderer.

He 'gave the 'answer `angrily.

The 'fellow's 'very `dangerous.

Mixed Patterns

A: 'Where were you 'going to `meet him?
B: At the 'door of the 'corner `pub.

A: And 'what were you 'going to `do?
B: We were 'going to 'have a `drink.

C: 'Why did you 'hit him on the `head?
D: Be'cause he be'gan to `fight me.
C: But 'why did you 'hit him so `hard?
D: 'Hitting him 'hard was a mis`take.

(d) *Falling Tone*
Statements
I'm 'not `hungry.

70

The po'lice are `questioning her.
To'morrow'll be 'too `late.
He 'hit the 'man on the `head.
You'd 'better 'come to the `pub with me.
You can 'ask at the 'shop on the `corner.
She 'didn't 'even 'take her `coat off.
I 'only 'want to 'ask you a few `questions.
He 'hit him on the 'head and 'stole his `money.
It's 'under the 'floor at the 'foot of his `bed.

Question-word questions
'Where's he `going?
'Why did it 'have to `happen?
'What's 'that 'piece of `paper?
'What 'kind of 'vote does he `want?
'Why did you al'low the 'boy to `do it?

Commands
'Don't 'leave us a`lone.
'Sit 'down on the `chairs.
'Get 'up and 'walk in front of `Tina.
'Drop your 'gun and 'put your `hands up.
'Tell me 'where you're 'hiding `Mike.

(e) *Rising Tone*
Questions
'Is there 'going to be a ´strike?
'Did you 'call the ´meeting?
'Did 'Reggie 'go to the po´lice?
'Do you 'think there'll be any ´violence?
'Did his 'wife 'get my ´message?
'Were you at the 'Trevors' 'house ´yesterday?
'Do you 'think they're 'really ´necessary?
You'd 'shoot me in the ´back?
There are 'no 'soldiers in the ´park?
You've for'gotten the 'ten 'hostages 'last De´cember?

(f) *Rising Tone Questions and Falling Tone Answers*

'Are you 'all ʼright?	ʼYes, I `am.
'Did you ʼsee him?	'No, I `didn't.
'Have the 'coppers ʼcaught him?	'No, they `haven't.
'Can't you 'see he 'isn't ʼwell?	ʼYes, I `can.
'Are you in 'love with 'Mike ʼStanding?	ʼYes, I `am.
'Has he 'offered to ʼmarry you?	'No, he `hasn't.
'Do you 'always do 'everything that he ʼsays?	ʼYes, we `do.
You 'saw her 'face when she 'heard the ʼnews?	ʼYes, I `did.
You 'think he's 'hiding 'Standing ʼhere?	ʼYes, I `do.
You 'knew that he 'stole the 'man's ʼmoney?	'No, I `didn't.

(g) *Rising Tone Question, Rising Tone Echo, Falling Tone Answer*

A: 'Is it ʼtrue?

B: ʼTrue? `Yes. It `is.

C: 'Is she your ʼgirlfriend?

D: My ʼgirlfriend? `No. she `isn't.

E: 'Is there 'going to be a ʼstrike?

F: A ʼstrike? `Yes. There `is.

G: 'Do you 'think 'Reggie will `win?

H: ʼReggie? `No. I `don't.

I: 'Have you 'ever 'seen ʼblood?

J: Blood? `Yes. Of `course.

(h) *Rising Tone followed by Falling Tone*

'If you 'go aʼgainst the ,Union, there'll be `trouble.

'If we 'want to 'go to ,work, 'nobody can `stop us.

As 'soon as 'Reggie 'opened his ,mouth, they `shouted.

'When the 'fight be,gan, you 'did `nothing.

'If there's ,trouble, they'll 'blame `you.

'While 'Reggie was ,passing, they `laughed at him.

'When I 'got 'back to the ,classroom, the 'children were 'standing on their `desks.

'If I ,tell them, 'hundreds of our 'soldiers will `die.

72

'If 'Hamish 'wasn't ,there, there 'wouldn't be 'any `trouble.
'When the po'lice ,come, I'll 'climb out of your `window.

(i) *Mixed Questions and Answers from the Plays*

MR FRASER: As 'soon as 'Reggie 'opened his ,mouth, they `shouted, they `threw things—

MARY: And 'you 'just ´stood there? You al'lowed it 'all to ´happen?

MR FRASER: `Yes.

MARY: And 'when the 'fight be,gan, 'you 'did ´nothing?

MR FRASER: `Nothing.

MARY: But `why, Dad?

BELLA: 'What was `that?

WIFE: A 'knock at the `window.

WAR MINISTER: My 'gun's in my `bedroom.

WIFE: 'Don't 'leave us a`lone. `Oh. 'Why 'aren't the `servants here?

BELLA: I'm 'sure it was the `wind. I'll 'go and `see.

WAR MINISTER: ,No. ,No. There , isn't any wind. I'll 'go my, self.—
`Tina. 'What are `you doing here?

MIKE: 'What did you `tell them?

BEN: `Nothing. 'Where were you 'going to 'meet `June?

MIKE: 'Outside the `cinema—the Ri`alto.

BEN: And 'only 'June ´knows?

MIKE: `Yes.

BEN: You lied to me. 'That 'blood on your 'shirt 'isn't `yours. 'Why did you `hit the old man?

MIKE: He be'gan to `shout. I was a`fraid.

BEN: 'Did the 'old 'man 'see your ´face?

MIKE: `No.